W9-CFQ-330

the Illuminated
PRAYER

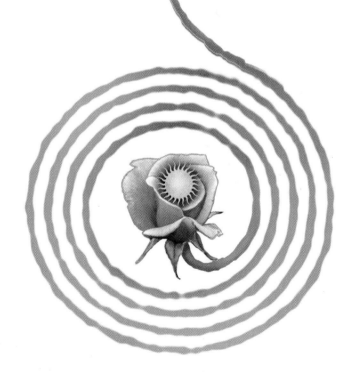

ال م

THE
ILLUMINATED PRAYER

THE
ILLUMINATED
PRAYER

THE FIVE-TIMES PRAYER OF THE SUFIS
AS REVEALED BY
JELLALUDIN RUMI & BAWA MUHAIYADDEEN

Coleman Barks   Michael Green

BALLANTINE WELLSPRING™

The Ballantine Publishing Group • New York

For Kabir and
the other light-bearers
of his generation

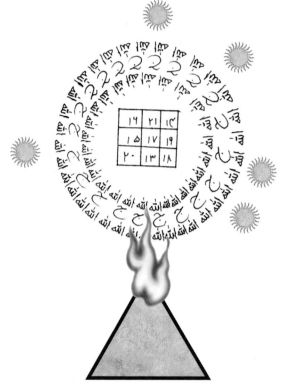

A Ballantine Wellspring™ Book
Published by The Ballantine Publishing Group
Copyright © 2000 by Coleman Barks and Michael Green
All rights reserved under International and Pan-American Copyright Conventions. Published in the United States
by The Ballantine Publishing Group, a division of Random House, Inc., New York, and simultaneously in Canada
by Random House of Canada Limited, Toronto.

Permission to quote the poems and works of Bawa Muhaiyaddeen was graciously given by the Bawa
Muhaiyaddeen Fellowship.

Ballantine is a registered trademark and Ballantine Wellspring™ and the Ballantine Wellspring™ colophon are
trademarks of Random House, Inc.

www.randomhouse.com/BB/

Library of Congress Catalog Card Number: 99-91634

ISBN 0-345-43545-1

Manufactured in the United States of America

First Edition: January 2000

10   9   8   7   6   5   4   3   2   1

Contents

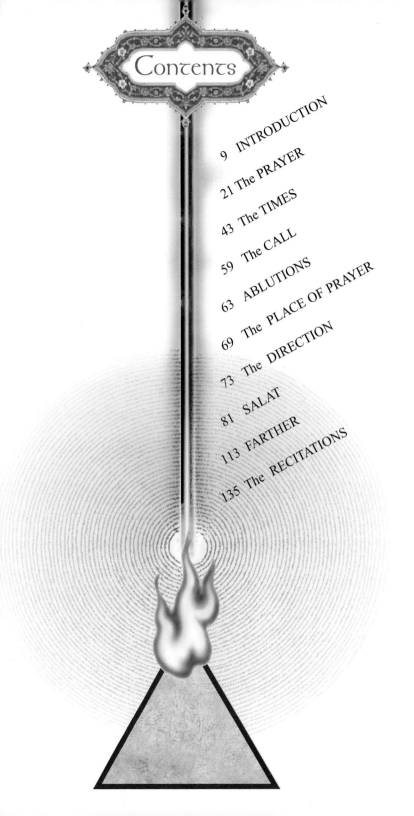

A Blessing

In the Sufi Way, endeavors are sanctified at their beginning with the words *Bismillah ir Rahman ir Raheem,*

IN THE NAME OF GOD,

BOUNDLESSLY COMPASSIONATE, BOUNDLESSLY MERCIFUL.

How wonderful that *mercy* and *compassion* are given as the essential textures of an all-transcending Creator. These nurturing qualities evoke a compelling Deity, *God the Mother Father.* In the gender-rich Arabic grammar, *Allah* is masculine, *Rahman* and *Raheem* feminine. And the root word of both *Rahman* and *Raheem* is *womb.*

The simple *Bismillah* at the top of the opposite page comes from a letter sent by the blessed Prophet. Below it is an illuminated *Bismin* rendered in Hebrew by the Sufi calligrapher Muhammad Abdul Kadir. It bears witness that the Prophet came, like blessed Jesus before him, as a truth-bearer and reviver in the ancient line of the Hebrew prophets. May their one song permeate this book!

ONE SONG

All religions,
all this singing,
is one song.

> The differences are just
> illusion and vanity.

The sun's light looks a little different
on this wall than it does on that wall,
and a lot different on this other one,
but it's still one light.

We have borrowed these clothes,
these time and place personalities,
from a light, and when we praise,
we're pouring them back in.

S PLITTING THE S TONE

hen my last book, *The Illuminated Rumi*, was finished at noon on the day of the deadline, my wife, Sally, and I had to hand-deliver the disks to our editor in New York City. The drive from Pennsylvania was a navigational disaster. An untested shortcut got us on the wrong expressway in rush hour; we finally landed in midtown Manhattan as night fell, frazzled by traffic and lateness. With no time to park, I went straight to the publisher's, pulled half onto the sidewalk, and headed into the building, leaving Sally in the car.

At that exact moment, a middle-aged man stepped under the building's cavernous entrance arch, unrolled a prayer mat, and with quiet dignity began the evening devotions of Salat, the Five-Times Prayer. *We had arrived right on cue.* It was a prophetic moment, though I did not catch it at the time.

—Michael Green

Introduction

I t's actually rather stunning to contemplate *regularly* breaking the momentum of our obsessive daily pursuits to center ourselves on the richness of our deepest *heart's desire*. But why not? *Split the stone and there am I.*

If *The Illuminated Prayer* is a teaching book, as its first student I know how important it is to see The Prayer through the lens of universality. Anything less creates more division. Coleman contributed a running commentary of his remarkable Rumi translations. Rumi's deep connection with our teacher Bawa Muhaiyaddeen unfolded as the book grew. Together, these two masters collaborated to guide this book, and may God's peace forever surround them.

Jellaludin Rumi was born at the beginning of the thirteenth century in an outer province of the Persian empire, in what is now Afghanistan. His father fled with his family before the threat of the invading Mongol hordes and wandered the Middle East until he was invited to teach at a religious college in Konya, Turkey. At his father's death, Rumi took over his position as head of the seminary community. Rumi was a popular scholar, a respected author, and an expert in mysticism. His life was by all accounts a success until the fall of 1244, when he met his awakener, a mysterious wandering dervish of blazing temperament, one of the hidden enlightened ones. Shams, whose name means *sun,* had traveled everywhere searching for someone who could "endure my company." One story of their encounter holds that Shams cast all of Rumi's books into a fountain, and at the younger's protest, he retrieved them dry and undamaged. Rumi promptly abandoned his comfortable honors and entered into a series of intense communion retreats with Shams. Finally, at the death of his beloved God-friend, Rumi became nothing, became everything, became the amphora's neck through which a great flood of transformational poetry poured into the world.

Our awakener was a sparrow of a man named **Bawa Muhaiyaddeen**, of whom less is actually known than Rumi. There are scattered encounters with Bawa around the turn of the century, but he firmly entered modern history in the forties, when he was discovered by pilgrims at a jungle shrine in Sri Lanka venerated by Hindus, Buddhists, Christians, and Muslims. He seemed immensely old, timeless, although his appearance was youthful and his skin as smooth as a child's. Bawa would always turn aside questions about his personal history, often with the reply that the only important story was God's story. Eventually, Bawa came to America and began a simple existence in a Philadelphia row house. He owned nothing, was owned by no one, and gave life to Rumi's words: *The Sufi opens his hands to the universe and gives away each instant, free. Unlike someone who begs on the street for money to survive, a dervish begs to give you his life.* He charged no fees, accepted no presents, and treated every seeker like family. Anyone present during mealtime was always invited to stay. He would ask the simple but spiritually galvanizing question: *What do you want?* Whatever the answer, Bawa would return it transformed. Jonathan Granoff tells of how he witnessed the workings of this Sufi guru during an afternoon session with two aspirants. The first seeker expressed a burning desire to know God. Bawa responded with a homespun Ayurvedic recipe for curing hemorrhoids. The second, looking for practical guidance in a minor family drama, was treated to a lofty dis-

cussion of highest perfect wisdom. Jon interviewed each afterward and found that Bawa had hit spectacular bull's-eyes. The first visitor indeed suffered from terrible hemorrhoids, and what he had felt was the utter relief that someone could completely see through all his defenses and posturing and still deeply care for him on every level. In that moment of psychic diagnosis, layers of shame dissolved; resistance to faith melted. Likewise, the second answer had found the crucial and unspoken question.

Bawa often broke into devotional song, entering into intimate conversation with a God who was at once transcendent, personal, and the deepest part of us. Slowly it dawned that in this person the purest Vedic nondual tradition was embracing purest Islam. In the great procession of spiritual revelation systems, Oldest wed Newest, not symbolically, but unitively and transformatively. Some great cycle was completed.

11

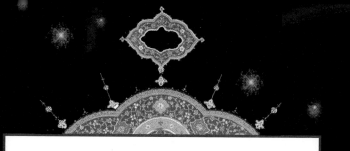

THE QUTB

Sufis define *Qutb* as a conjoining of the magnetic axis of the cosmos and the spiritual axis of human consciousness. When a renewer of the Way is needed, the Qutb wisdom-field can appear as a person. Working deeply in the river of human events, the Qutb is sometimes hidden, sometimes not, but always known to the community of saints. As a historical figure, the Qutb may parallel the Avatars of Vedic tradition. *By all evidence Jellaludin Rumi and Bawa Muhaiyaddeen were Qutbs.*

Both taught with an oceanic tide of words: Rumi produced a vast body of poetry; Bawa was a living Thousand and One Nights. There were talks and stories, and stories within stories, songs, accounts of mystic journeys, and an endless supply of droll folktales. Lots of ego-disabling laughter kept things loose. But this was abundance with an edge: when the sluice gates were open and pouring, the sudden realization would come that you were trying to catch a torrent from the Other Side in a mental thimble! Rumi said it: *The way of love is not a subtle argument. The door there is devastation.*

The Qutb's work is to expose a patch of yielding soil where a well might be dug. Ours is to become a kind of life that sips only from its wisdom-water.

You are water, we are plants.
You are fullness, we're empty.
You speak. We are the sound of your different voices.
You're the search,
        Why aren't we found?

When we resisted, preferring the solid predictability of our old inertial intelligence, his teaching could turn as paradoxical as a Zen koan. The sudden clap of thunder and the room was full of heads flying off shoulders. We needed new heads, ones that could hold both a night sky and brilliant daylight in their sight at once. *The Qutb confuses the mind to strengthen the soul.*

The metaphysical environment into which The Prayer was introduced was outside the tangled accretions of history. It was a place where *Islam* didn't mean a religion or culture or even a belief system, but a bright burning state with a quicksilver universality too elusive and grand for anyone's ownership. *"Everything is Islam. Islam is the spotless purity of the heart, it is a vast ocean. If God's teaching is there, it is Islam. To act out the qualities of truth and embrace with true love, that is Islam. The tired hearts, the hurt ones, to embrace them with love, and give them the milk of love, embrace them face-to-face, heart-to-heart, in unity, that is Islam.* Only much later did we learn that Bawa was only repeating how the words *Islam* and *Muslim* first fell from the lips of the holy Prophet. Fresh from mystical dimensions, they meant "man's self-surrender to God" and "one who surrendered himself to God," *apparently without limiting their compass to any specific community.* In the third sura, or passage, of the Quran, for instance, Abraham is spoken of as having *"surrendered himself unto God"* (kana muslim), and later the disciples of Jesus say, *"Bear thou witness that we have surrendered ourselves unto God"* (bi-anna muslim).

Bawa Muhaiyaddeen would not claim *spotless purity* for himself, only that God alone knows our hearts. And Bawa did not like the way labels create divisions today. To indicate "what" he was, he would relate the many years he had traveled the world mastering the other religions, explaining that he had now become *a student of Islam* because he understood that it was the final revelation of a great cycle of revelations.

When a child asked him one day what to say when asked what religion she was, Bawa gave another hint of how his community might understand itself:

You are a Christian because you believe in Jesus, and you are a Jew because you believe in all the prophets including Moses. You are a Muslim because you believe in Muhammad as a prophet, and you are a Sufi because you believe in the universal teaching of God's love. You are really none of those, but you are all of those because you believe in God. And once you believe in God, there is no religion. Once you divide yourself off with religions, you are separated from your fellowman.

From a twelfth-century illumination
showing Muslims, Christians, and Jews sitting in the lap of Abraham.

The angels are said to be in constant adoration of the divine.

By all accounts, Rumi was devoted to the practice of the Salat. Bawa introduced it toward the end of his teaching in the West. For Rumi's disciples, no introduction was necessary, but for most of us the practice was all new. Was it an obligation or an invitation? Somehow the community managed to embrace both possibilities at once. In the open space of the heart, the contradiction didn't amount to much. Self-discipline is an essential part of the spiritual landscape, and obligations—with no wiggle room—can be useful tools to tame our more churlish elements. But Bawa was keenly aware of how quickly liberation systems with rigid marching orders turn into a dumb obsession with other people's behavior. "God gives us alarm clocks," said Gurdjieff, "then we fall asleep dreaming of alarm clocks."

Today a whole generation has what Bawa called "light minds"—a new kind of transparent intellect that is smart, wary of all authority, wired into the information age: *See all, hear all, accept nothing.* Deluged with shuck, light minds are ever alert for the authentic fragrance, and easily grasp subtle understandings once the domain of mystics. Such a mind has to be approached gingerly, with a carrot, not a stick. Bawa Muhaiyaddeen was the master of this. Meeting him, one instantly knew he was half in the drama, half gone: gone beyond language, beyond systems—beyond anything in the realm of form. There was no agenda, only a deep pool of compassion.

LOOKING, WE DO NOT SEE IT; REACHING, WE CANNOT TOUCH IT.

Subtle understandings

17

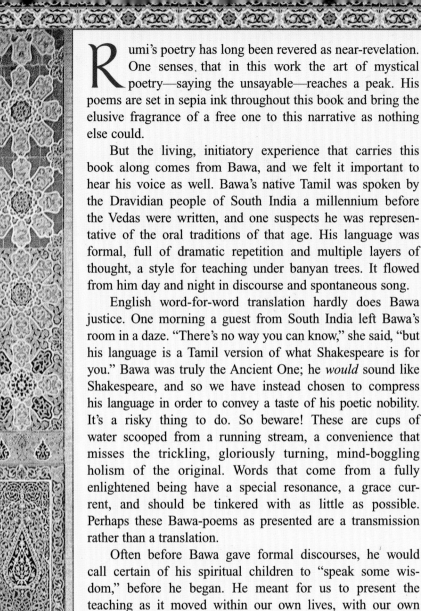

Rumi's poetry has long been revered as near-revelation. One senses, that in this work the art of mystical poetry—saying the unsayable—reaches a peak. His poems are set in sepia ink throughout this book and bring the elusive fragrance of a free one to this narrative as nothing else could.

But the living, initiatory experience that carries this book along comes from Bawa, and we felt it important to hear his voice as well. Bawa's native Tamil was spoken by the Dravidian people of South India a millennium before the Vedas were written, and one suspects he was representative of the oral traditions of that age. His language was formal, full of dramatic repetition and multiple layers of thought, a style for teaching under banyan trees. It flowed from him day and night in discourse and spontaneous song.

English word-for-word translation hardly does Bawa justice. One morning a guest from South India left Bawa's room in a daze. "There's no way you can know," she said, "but his language is a Tamil version of what Shakespeare is for you." Bawa was truly the Ancient One; he *would* sound like Shakespeare, and so we have instead chosen to compress his language in order to convey a taste of his poetic nobility. It's a risky thing to do. So beware! These are cups of water scooped from a running stream, a convenience that misses the trickling, gloriously turning, mind-boggling holism of the original. Words that come from a fully enlightened being have a special resonance, a grace current, and should be tinkered with as little as possible. Perhaps these Bawa-poems as presented are a transmission rather than a translation.

Often before Bawa gave formal discourses, he would call certain of his spiritual children to "speak some wisdom," before he began. He meant for us to present the teaching as it moved within our own lives, with our own images, not simply to repeat his words. He wanted words to flow spontaneously from a place deeper than the intellect.

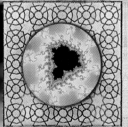
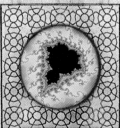
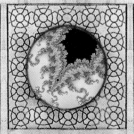
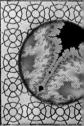

When everything fell into place, we would listen to our own words with as much interest as the assembly.

To represent the master was Sufi basic training. Bawa didn't hesitate to correct us right in midsentence. But when our focus was right, we slipped into the ancient process of *transmission*. Light-bringers come and pass on what they can. If something is lost, something is gained. The vastness of an enlightened being like Bawa or Rumi can never be even remotely comprehended by a student, but we are guided to certain aspects of the whole that we try to make our own, and to which we bring the richness of our own gifts. If the process is successful, we begin to display portions of the original picture with a worthy depth of detail and complexity. Like a fractal zoom, the same essential patterns will appear again and again, always different, always the same.

Bawa said that a great wisdom-tree that had grown in the East had fallen to the West. This examination of an ancient prayer form can be thought of as a slender shoot growing from one of its fruits. The seed is bursting with vitality, but is still in the process of adapting to the new soil. Like that, we have endeavored to stay true to the essential teachings, even while finding new ways to convey them. It is our hope that these pages lead, like tracks in the sand, to something deeper than postures and recitations. May they lead to the initiatory atmosphere of the Qutb.

> *The Prayer is an excellent act, but*
> *its spirit and meaning are*
> *more excellent than its form, even*
> *as the human spirit is more excellent and*
> *more enduring*
> *than the form. For the human form*
> *does not abide forever, but the spirit does.*
> *In the same way, the form of The Prayer does not remain,*
> *but its meaning and spirit do.*

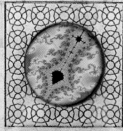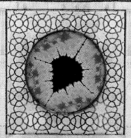

Let yourself
be silently drawn
by the
stronger pull

of what

you really

love.

—Rumi

Sun images appear throughout this book as symbols of the one great brightness. Rumi and Bawa both loved the sun for its magnanimous gifting of light and warmth to all without distinction. As an emblem for the front of our meeting hall, Bawa designed a great sun with an "Allah-hu" in its center, and had me draw its rays shifting through every color of the rainbow.

The Prayer

What is it that we *really love*? What is the *stronger pull*?

Behavioral scientists believe that immediately after birth, we enjoy a happy blurring of the distinction between "self" and "nonself," but that before too long in our life-trajectory, we pull ourselves free of such oceanic unity and we *individuate*. It's a fascinating new experience: *Me!* Years go by, life experience accumulates. We slowly discover that our self-entity exists within an atmosphere of aloneness and *separation*. Our first instinct is to break out of the isolation with a lot of grasping and possessing—friends, lovers, food, cars, money, land, whatever. We try to dull the ache with entertainment, understand it with philosophy, or accept it in therapy. No matter. Nothing quite delivers the abiding wholeness we sense is *really the way we ought to be*.

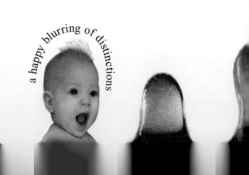

a happy blurring of distinctions

The human shape is a ghost
    made of distraction and pain.
        Sometimes pure light, sometimes cruel,
           trying wildly to open,
                this image tightly held within itself.

Aloneness

and

Separation

Fascinating
Experience

At
some point,
when we
get far
enough away, perhaps
even lost in the outer darknesses,
we tire of listening to our
own lies. We open another
ear. *A call is heard.*

"The mystics are gathering
in the street. Come out!"

"Leave me alone. I'm sick."

"I don't care if you're dead! Jesus is here,
and he wants to resurrect somebody!"

An intuition is awakened within us of the original human experience, of a deep, effortless unity, not with *things*, but with the *ocean of pure love-being* within which they exist. A longing and a thirst . . .

The thirst in our souls is the attraction put out by water itself.

We belong to it, and it to us.

25

. . . and a new attraction is felt, a tidal pull toward something deep and unknown. Something shifts inside. Rumi says

be like a fish on a beach moving toward wave-sound.

The Prayer and the teachings here are tools to nourish and strengthen this pull, this

We can't help being thirsty
moving toward the voice
of water.
     Milk-drinkers draw close
to the mother, Muslims, Christians,
Jews, Buddhists, Hindus, shamans,
    everyone hears the intelligent sound
       and moves, with thirst, to meet it.

nging to return to the Source

The teachings in this book are part of an ancient Way of *returning*. They go far back before recorded history. The Way is not "religion," it is the root from which all religions grow.

Signs of this Way can be found everywhere, among all peoples. The Way exists to serve, and chameleon-like, it takes much of its external coloration from whatever culture or religion it finds itself in.

In the world of mystic Islam, the ones who embrace and transmit this way of returning, of knowing themselves, are often called *Sufis*.

Their "I" is not what most think of as "I."

I am cloud and rain being released,
and then the meadow as it soaks it in.

I wash the grains of mortality
from the cloth around a dervish.

I am the rose of eternity, not made of
water or fire or the wandering wind,
or even earth. I play with those.

I am
a light within his light. If you see me, be
careful. Tell no one what you've seen.

The "I" that so many have defended to their dying breath might be likened to a slightly unstable computer operating system. It's got wonderful features, but it still crashes and needs regular upgrades. Ultimately it is nothing more than a swarm of charged particles, or rather, it's only *the pattern* of charges, completely ephemeral, subject at any moment to error messages, erasure, viruses, random power surges . . . even *unfixable crashes.* The Sufi's response to such a marginal existence is simple: abandon the assumption that this *program* is who we really are. Marvelous things can now happen. We might identify with wider horizons—like the hard drive, or the processor. Or the network, the World Wide Web, the wide world, or finally, *the great sea of being* supporting everything.

This opening up of identity is the great work, and no effort in it is ever wasted. Those who find their way to the shore of this sea are ennobled and transformed. Those diving in discover they are no different from the sea. They were God's secret. Now God is their secret.

> Dissolver of sugar, dissolve me,
> if this is the time.
> Do it gently with a touch of hand, or a look.
> Every morning I wait at dawn. That's when it
> happened before.
> Or do it suddenly like an execution. How else
> can I get ready for death?
>
> You breathe without a body like a spark.
> You grieve, and I begin to feel lighter.
> You keep me away with your arm,
> but the keeping away is pulling me in.

Where do we begin? The arts of starting out, of soul-turning, of returning to the vast bright waters of universal consciousness are all found in the realm of prayer.

GREETINGS FROM THE SHORES OF MYSTIC OBLIVION

wicker basket sank in the Ocean,
aw itself full of seawater,
   decided it could live independently.
    Left the ocean,

nd not a drop stayed in it.

But the ocean took it back.
For God's sake, stay near the sea!
Walk the beach.
Your face is pale.

I am sinking in the ocean of this subject.

31

A man in prison receives a prayer rug from a friend. What he had wanted, of course, was a file or a crowbar or a key! But he began using the rug, doing the Five-Times Prayer before dawn, at noon, midafternoon, after sunset, and before sleep. Bowing, sitting up, bowing again, he notices an odd pattern in the weave of the rug at the point where his head touches. He studies and meditates on that pattern, gradually discovering that it is a diagram of the lock that confines him to his cell and how it works. He's able to escape.

Anything you do every day
can open
into the deepest spiritual place,
which is freedom.

What nine months does for the embryo
Forty early mornings will do
for your growing awareness.

There is no single word in English that conveys the scope of the Arabic word *Salat*. "Prayer," "blessings," "supplication," and "grace" are implied, but all fail to convey the Salat's marvelous integration of devotional heart-surrender with physical motion. In Salat, our entire being is engaged in a single luminous event.

Throughout this book, The Prayer will mean Salat and all its resonances.

The Salat that we practice begins with the *Miraj*, the mystic Night Journey of the noble prophet Muhammad. Called from his meditation into superconsciousness, he ascends through the heavens and beyond to mingle and merge with the Lord and Creator, light upon Light.

On his journey, the Prophet contemplates the angels in their ceaseless attitudes of awe and praise.

R eturning, he brings back the earthly forms of these celestial adorations. The Prayer is gifted not to one tribe or to one race or one religion but to

all humanity, and we present it here as such, a treasure for everyone.

Moving with The Prayer as response to *inner need* draws one into the precious community of mystic lovers everywhere.

As witnessed by his companions, the early Salat led by the Holy Prophet reflected his intimate contact with divine presence. It had all the irregularities, additions, and subtractions of a dynamic living transmission. The congregation followed the Prophet, the Prophet flowed with God. Eventually a predictable pattern emerged.

At the Call,

says the Book of Revelation,

*leave your trading and
hasten unto remembrance.*

The Prayer lends a new life to the day, binding it into the rhythm of a sacred circle. Like a waterwheel that ceaselessly catches water out of a stream and spills it into a garden, The Prayer lifts us up again and again out of our preoccupations and sets us into a sacred time. The Prayer empowers us to put aside the ten thousand cares and realign to the unity and blessedness intrinsic to all things.

Be courageous and discipline yourself.
Work. Keep digging your well.
Don't think about getting off from work.
Water is there somewhere.
Submit to a daily practice.
Your loyalty to that
is a ring on the door.
Keep knocking, and the joy inside
will eventually open a window
and look out to see who's there.

The Prayer is a deep psychological force field to help us overcome our molelike resistances to the light. The Prayer is an unfolding series of archetypal motions and gestures that appear in endless variation throughout all the devotional practices of the human family.

Salat is a remarkably compact and focused exercise. It gently returns our lives to "that which we really love" five times every day, and grounds that returning in the movements and knowledge of body-wisdom.

*The body itself is a screen
to shield and partially reveal
the light that's blazing
inside your presence.*

Following celestial law, the earth each day performs a complete turning. The light moves through five stages as the sun dawns, climbs to its zenith, descends downward in the slanting rays of afternoon, sets in glowing colors, and disappears into darkness. For the Sufi, this cycle is a mirror of the human life span: our dawning into the world, our growth, maturation, decline, and death. In these five stages, the soul makes its journey around another sun that never rises or sets.

The Prayer invites us to awaken from the superficial self at these moments of the day. By aligning our devotional work with these natural times of power we start to move with the rhythms of God's creation in a new way, attuned to the mystical correspondences between outer and inner and to the seasons of life.

Think of how PHENOMENA come trooping
out of the Desert of Non-existence
into this materiality.
　　　　　Morning and night,
they arrive in a long line and take over
from each other, "It's my turn now. Get out!"

A son comes of age, and the father packs up.
This place of phenomena is a wide exchange
of highways, with everything going all sorts
of different ways.
　　　　　We seem to be sitting still,
but we're actually moving, and the Fantasies
of Phenomena are sliding through us
like ideas through curtains.

The Times

MAY THIS INTENTION BE FULFILLED

The Five Times of Prayer are linked with the five elemental forces of Earth, Fire, Water, Air, and Ether. These five forces fit within a grand *living* cosmology, and to get inside it we must slip the mechanistic world outlook that imprisons the soul. We must contemplate what Bawa called *the Beginningless Beginning,* a dimension that is not so much *before* time as *outside* time, and so is also *now*. This is a deep-water teaching of the Qutb. It is not ordinary information, and we must enter it as a drifting out to sea, as a glimpse through blue green waters at ancient truth-currents no tongue can describe. It is an account told by one who never lies, who can never find words to hold its ineffable truth.

Out of the profound silence of the beginningless beginning
a Divine Longing arises:

I was a Hidden Treasure and I desired to be known.

In response to this Original Intention, a great light upwells from within the Longing, and God beholds it as the beautiful radiance of His own face. This is the *Nur Muhammad, pure consciousness aware of itself.*

The moment Allah gazes upon this light, all the mysteries that had lain dormant burst from within Him as rays of sparkling luminosity. These are the souls of all creation, and they settle on the primordial elements: earth, fire, water, air, and ether, permeating them with living consciousness.

But by nature these five forces are inimical to each other: water drowning fire, fire scorching earth, and so with the rest. Then Allah places before them the Nur, shining with the radiance of the full moon, resonating with the Great Truth: THERE IS NO COHERENCE, NO MEANING, NO OTHER CENTER BUT GOD. The elements bow in reverence and humility. Forsaking pride of otherness, they are fused into a whole by the compelling beauty and energy of the Nur. *Chaos* becomes *Cosmos*.

The archetypal relationship between creation and Creator is established, a ceaseless flow of adoration and praise. In this field, all things flower. This is called *Awwal*, the Sphere of the Souls.

O God! You are the infinite open ray of light.
You alone are God, transcending everything,
You are all that Adam must become.
You are the tiny seed and the great universe.
You are the refuge, You are the path.

You are the handhold, You are the strength.
You are formlessness, You are form.
You are the bud and the fully opened flower.
You are the jeweled light within the eyes.

44

glimpse through blue green waters at ancient truth-currents no tongue can describe.

From Awwal, our souls descend from pure adoration into the dense realm of forgetfulness—*our world*— and become buried in the form of the body, "the shadow of God's love." Here the story of The Hidden Treasure unfolds once more. Just as the Nur emerged from within God, so the Nur must also emerge from concealment within the human heart.

When the soul first put on the body's shirt,
the ocean lifted up all its gifts.
When love first tasted the lips
of being human, it started singing.
We're from a country beyond this universe, yet our best guess is
we're made of earth and ashes.
We go knocking on strangers' doors to find out who we are.
We search this world for the great untying
of what was wed to us with birth
and gets undone at dying.

Eventually, when our longing grows deep enough, it brings us into the presence of a clarifying intelligence whose task it is to recover the hidden treasure, the "deep truth within a lie." This is our innate guide, the Qutb. Our scattered thinking and unfulfilled desires resist, but the nature of the Guide is irresistible love.

Why not become fresh from the gentleness of the heart-spring?
Why not laugh like a rose? Why not spread perfume?

In the supremely human act of submitting to the Guide, the work of release begins. As the separative dynamic of our elemental impulses is understood, the need to be a unified Self becomes an obligation spreading through our life. Innate wisdom begins to cleanse the heart of impurities so that the radiant brilliance of the *Nur Muhammad* may shine forth. In the presence of this higher organizing principle of light, the elements become a creative matrix of life.

In the end, the hidden treasure of the Nur is finally known *on earth as it is in heaven.* The veils dividing Creator and creation, seer and seen, fall away.

THE REAL WORK OF THE FIVE TIMES
Conflict among the five elements obscures the unifying impulse of love. Each element rules certain mental and emotional energies and, according to the teachings of the Qutb, exerts its greatest negative influence during a particular time of day. At these times The Prayer is most effective in transforming these elemental forces.

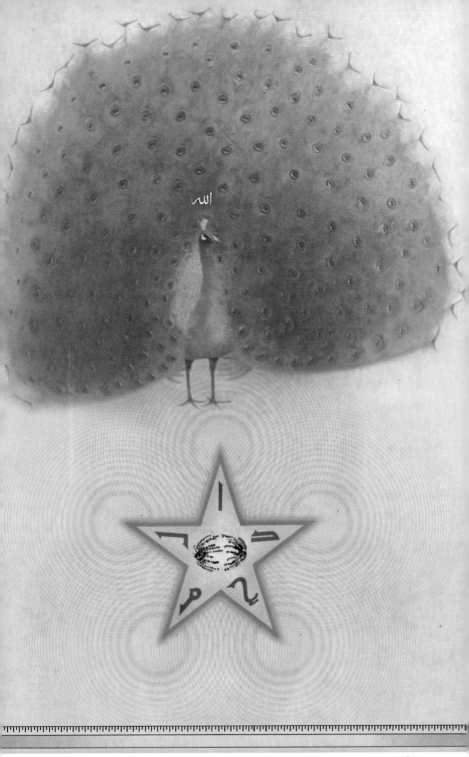

ur Muhammad, sometimes symbolized as a radiant peacock, unites the five conflicting elements into a creative matrix of life.

Ꝺꜳꝟꞁ Pꞃꜳyꞇꞃ
(called *Fajr*)

Dawn Prayer comes in the sacred hour before sunrise when a thread of light appears on the horizon. The angelic dimension moves into intimate contact with the ordinary world now, and anyone alert senses a remarkably sweet silence in the airwaves: Breezes stir, birds wake into song, and pilgrims arise. Keeping this prayer loosens the earthy torpor that lies heavily upon us at this hour. Earth is the realm of attachments to *form*: our own bodies, our possessions, our blood ties and lusts. Earth energies are born at the base of the spine. If they remain there, we stay fascinated with the things of the world, fearful of change and loss. Fajr releases these grasping earth obsessions into the flowing generosity of dawn.

The breeze at dawn has secrets to tell you.
Don't go back to sleep.
You must ask for what you really want.
Don't go back to sleep.
People are going back and forth across the doorsill
where the two worlds touch.
The door is round and open,
Don't go back to sleep.

NOON PRAYER
(called *Zuhr*)

Noon Prayer comes just *after* the sun has reached its greatest height in the sky. Fiery power is at its peak, stimulating abundant movement, growth, creativity, and forgetfulness. Human beings are engaged in what Rumi calls *desire-singing and rage-ranting, the elaborate language of personality.* Elemental fire is centered in the belly and manifests as anger, arrogance, and impatience. Persistent turning to inwardness at this time can transform these wild, surging energies into a passionate search for God. Our spiritual fire is fearlessly intent on annihilating the separate "I" and burning up resistances. *You are burning up your soul / to keep the body delighted,* says Rumi, *but you don't know what you are doing. / I am another kind of fire.*

> A candle is made to become
> entirely flame.
> In that annihilating moment
> it has no shadow.
>
> It is nothing but a tongue of light
> describing a refuge.
>
> Look at this
> just-finishing candle stub
> as someone who is finally safe
> from virtue and vice,
>
> The pride and the shame
> we claim from those.

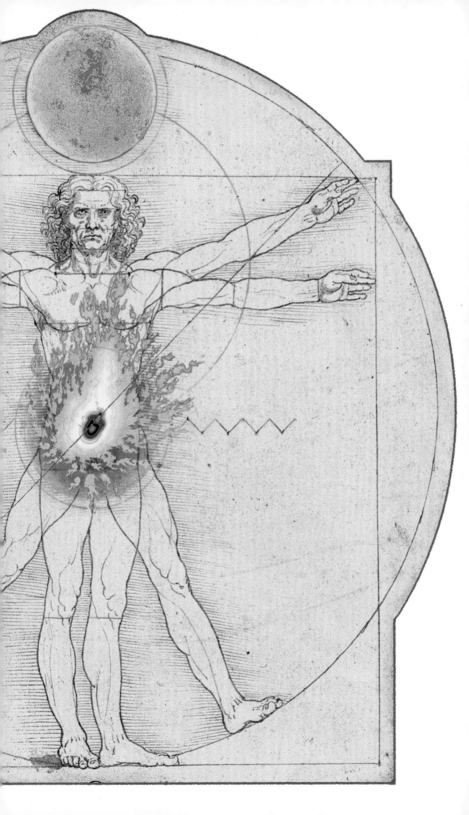

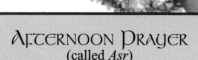

AFTERNOON PRAYER
(called *Asr*)

Afternoon Prayer comes when the sun has dropped halfway to the horizon and the length of an object's shadow is twice its height. Every day mirrors the sweep of a lifetime; lengthening shadows now signal the midlife time of crisis. An easy flow into swirling waters of life beckons and each must consciously choose to persevere on the Way of union. The time of lengthening shadows is the domain of the watery element. Its energies flood our emotional body as turbulent affairs of the heart. On a more subtle level water fascinates us with a vaporous pantheon of spirit guides and spiritual fantasies. The heart is alternately buffeted, perplexed, or seduced by tides of feeling. Desire and fantasy intermingle with genuine soul-longing. Prayer at this time calms this watery confusion. The Qutb says: *To complete Asr, we must understand the distinction between becoming one with God, or becoming one with the world.*

Rumi said, "A secret is hidden in the rhythms of music. If I revealed it, it would upset the world." One afternoon a musician was playing the violin and Rumi was listening with great concentration. A friend entered and said, "Stop this. They are announcing the Afternoon Prayer." "No," said Rumi, "this is also the Afternoon Prayer. Both talk to God."

EVENING PRAYER
(called *Maghrib*)

Evening Prayer comes after the sun has disappeared over the horizon and the clouds have lost their redness. The business of the day is completed, and quiet returns to the world. As mirrored in the span of a lifetime, this is the age of ripened maturity, when the strength of the body is waning, and darkness draws closer. Yet the mind is still restless and unhumbled. The element air governs mentation and unpredictable thought. Turning to prayer at this time grounds us in what is real and unchanging, and cuts our elemental attachments to mental airiness. The thoughts and theories of the day are released into proper perspective, along with the illusion of human will. Of the sunset prayer, Qutb Muhaiyaddeen says, *It is the time when the darkness of the world is dispelled by wisdom.*

A chunk of dirt thrown into the air breaks into pieces.
If you don't try to fly,
and so break yourself apart,
you will be broken open by death,
when it's too late for all you could become.

Leaves get yellow. The tree puts out fresh roots
and makes them green.
Why are you so content with a love
that turns you yellow?

Night Prayer
(called *Isha*)

Night Prayer comes about an hour after sunset, when stars are bright and the deep of night has settled over the earth. In the life cycle, night prayer comes at the time of death, the time of Jesus, the soul of man. This is when the body is laid in the earth and the soul continues its journey. Solidity falls away, but the spacious quality of ether grows, hypnotizing us with twinkling illusion. Turning to prayer at Isha erodes this elemental fascination with etheric phenomena, inclines us once more toward the *other* direction, where we are neither attracted nor repelled, where the *seer* and the *seen* become one, *and God alone is real.*

The Sufi's goal is to master the last prayer, the night prayer, before the body dies, and so *to die before death*.

Prayer goes deep at night.
Images dissolve. There's only God, and
silence, kindness, and grace.

The Call

Forget your life. Say
God is Great.
Get up!
You think you know what time it is . . .
It's time to pray.
You've created so many little idols,
too many.
Don't knock on any random door,
like a beggar. Reach your long hand out
to another door, beyond
where you go on the street.
The street where everyone says
How are you?
and no one says
How aren't you?

One of the most memorable sounds in devotional community is the Call to Prayer. It is said the Call is not merely an announcement that the time of prayer has arrived, it's an invitation God extends to the family of man through their own voice. Give the Call aloud to cleanse the consciousness-field. The hands are cupped behind the ears, a strangely natural position that blocks distractions and focuses attention.

The Call penetrates unseen worlds, summoning not only the faithful, but angelic beings from other dimens[...]

God is Greatest!
Allahu Akbar
(four times)

I bear witness
that there is no reality
apart from Supreme Reality
Ashhaddu al la illaha il Allah
(two times)

I bear witness
that Muhammad is the
radiant-heart messenger of God
Ashhaddu anna Muhammadan Rasulullah
(two times)

Come, come to Salat
Hayya ala-s-Salat
(two times)

Come, come to the highest
spiritual realization
Hayya ala-l-falah
(two times)

God is Greatest!
Allahu Akbar
(two times)

Nothing exists apart from Allah
La illaha il Allah

Sufis are not particularly interested in history, and this witnessing is more than the acknowledgment of a noble figure who left footprints in desert sand 1,400 years ago. It embraces a radiant light-guide that is now and ever shall be, the living light of the *Nur Muhammad*. Bawa was once asked, "What is the relationship between God, Muhammad, and myself?" He replied, *Imagine yourself as an orange. Muhammad is the juice, God is the taste.*

e have heard the call and begin the turning of our attention away from surface matters.

An orchard in fall, fruit trees
full and the vines plump.

A man sits there with his head
on his knee, eyes closed.

His friend says,
"Why stay sunk in mystical meditation
when the world is like this?
Such visible grace."
He replies, "That outer is
an elaboration of this inner. I prefer the origin."

Natural beauty is a tree limb
reflected in the water of a creek,
quivering there, not there.
The growing
that moves in the soul is more real.

We turn toward what the early Christians called *Philokalia,* or "the beautiful-good," what a Navajo sings of in his Blessingway, *Beauty above me, beauty below me, beauty before me, beauty behind me.*

To prepare ourselves to walk into spiritual beauty, we perform ablutions, the rite of purification, or *wudu.* We join with all the great traditions in honoring the power of water to renew the spirit while washing away the grime of the world.

We begin by setting our intention: a simple, essential sentiment springing from the heart will focus spiritual life into the purifications that follow. Worshipers dedicate their ablutions with the *Bismillah.*

Ablutions

One God   Many Names

The Ablutions fall into an easy natural sequence. Each action is done three times, with an appropriate blessing.

- Wash the hands to the wrists:
  May these hands be instruments of peace.

- Then cup a handful of water to the lips with the right hand, rinsing the mouth three times:
  May this mouth speak only the pleasing words,
  the healing words, the truthful words.

- Then lightly snuff water into the nose three times, which has a remarkably brightening effect on the senses:
  May I long for the sweet fragrance of sanctity.

- Then wash the whole face and eyes:
  May this face shine with the light of compassion.
  May these eyes see the work of the Creator
  everywhere they look.

- Run damp and refreshing hands over the top of the head. Pass the wet tips of the fingers inside and outside the ears, and over the nape of the neck:
  May these ears hear only the resonance of the
  Creator; may this neck bend in humility to the One.

- Wash the feet up to the ankles:
  May these feet walk on holy ground.

I first understood ablutions when I was traveling through Persia. I was sleeping in a courtyard, when a whole family came and did ablutions in the cistern. Then they were up and down all night, praying, talking, praying, I don't know what. It was so natural and joyous I knew I had a connection.

—Maryam Kabeer

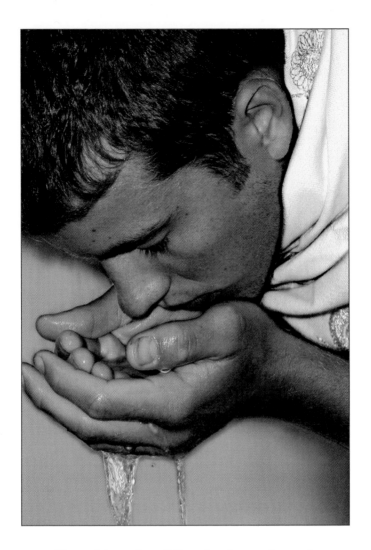

Your spirit needs to follow the changes happening
in the spacious place it knows about.

There, the scene is always new,
a clairvoyant river of picturing,
more beautiful than any on earth.

This is where the Sufis wash.
Purify your eyes, and see the pure world.
Your life will fill with radiant forms.

It's a question of cleaning
and then developing the spiritual senses.

TRUE ABLUTIONS

When you are performing your ablutions,
it is not merely washing your hands and feet. That
is not the real point, washing eyes, ears—
The purpose of washing each of these parts of your body is
that it gives you time, bit by bit, part by part,
> *to move your awareness away from the world*
> > *and toward God.*

Time to say within your heart,
> *I am now going to establish a connection with God.*
> *I am going to turn toward God.*
> *I am going to hand over my responsibilities, my love, to God.*

The blessed Prophet, may God's peace be upon him, said,
"While doing your ablutions, you must be aware only of your love for God.
Make your heart steadfast in that state."

This determination must become strong
through the process of your ablutions.
By the time you have finished, you must have
the intent and the aim of seeing God.
> *Nothing else.*
It doesn't matter, then, whether your eyes
are opened or if your eyes are closed.
> *God is all you will see whether they are opened or closed.*
This is the point when you can really call prayer surrender.

The day you succeed in these ablutions, your prayer becomes fruitful!
> *Then it is fulfilled.*
> *Then it is what we can call True Prayer.*
If you can make this state steadfast in yourself,
> *then not one second of your prayer will be wasted.*
Then your prayer will be The Prayer of completeness.
When you have that prayer, when such a prayer is made,
every part of it is a contract with God.

Then your eyes won't draw you away. Your ears won't draw you away.
> *Only He will be drawing you, and you will be drawing Him.*

This is the connection you will have. This is the true prayer.

ABLUTIONS

BY THE TIME YOU HAVE FINISHED, YOU MUST HAVE

THE INTENT AND THE AIM

OF SEEING GOD.

NOTHING ELSE.

The Place of Prayer

For those who have come to grow,
The whole world is a garden.
For those who wish to remain in the dream,
the whole world is a stage.
For those who have come to learn,
the whole world is a university.
For those who have come to know God,
the whole world is a prayer mat.

—From the teachings of
Bawa Muhaiyaddeen

In this prayer no special sanctuary is needed. Little space is required for Face-to-Face Seeing, just a clean area in which a prayer mat can fit. Magnificent buildings have been raised for prayer, but Sufis build with something more permanent than baked brick and lime: We are raising a mosque of indestructible light in the inner quarters of the heart. A teaching:

The Qutb asked, *If the world is a place to grow, what are you?*
I am the farmer.
No, you are the earth; I am the farmer. I am the one who will clear your thickets and thorns and plant sweet orchards! But if the world is a theater, what are you?
Then I am the stage, and you are the actor.
And if the world is a place to learn?
Then I am the school and you are the student.
And if the world is a place to pray?
Then you are The Prayer and I am The Prayer mat.

THE FAR MOSQUE

The place that Solomon made
      to worship in,
called the Far Mosque, is not
      built of earth
and water and stone, but of
      intention and wisdom
and mystical conversation and
      compassionate action.

Every part of it is intelligent and
      responsive
to every other. The carpet bows
      to the broom.
The door knocker and the door
      swing together
like musicians. This heart sanctuary
      does exist,
      but it can't be described. Why try?

DOES EXIST · CAN'T BE DESCRIBED

The Sufi compass points unwaveringly to a unified field of divine consciousness *within which* the multiplicity of the world *appears*. The eye looking in *this* direction sees profound singleness, sees all humankind as *one* family, sees all prayer as a turning this way. As symbol and focus of this unity, we have been given the ancient shrine of the Kaaba. We are all familiar with scenes of pilgrims circling this mysterious black cube, bowing in unison—with millions more around the world turning toward it five times a day in great planetary waves.

A single geographical direction for Prayer transforms the entire planet into one vast place of prayer. But ultimately, we face not to a direction within the universe, but toward the place of surrender, the inner heart. True unity moves from the *inner outward*. It may be reflected by a sublime external order, but soul freedom is rarely won by outside arrangements. Facing the Direction is a subtle matter; it opens the eye that in the many sees the One.

The history of the Kaaba yields rich mythological understandings. It reaches down to the roots of human experience, to the exile of Adam and Eve. Outside the Garden, as the history goes, the primeval couple part ways, and alone, each wanders the outer realm, the world of sickness, old age, and death.

As parents of the human family, Adam and Eve are also embodiments of the two sides of human nature: receptive and creative, spirit and body, yin and yang. Their story is a timeless mystery-drama in the inner world, and their estrangement is a split in our lives as well, a crisis the I Ching calls "Stagnation." *The male principle draws farther and farther away, while the female principle sinks farther into the depths. Heaven and earth are out of communion and all things are benumbed. What is above has no relation to what is below, and on earth confusion and disorder prevail.*

The Direction

In vain the pair searches the world for a place of comfort. At last, repentance is awakened, the light of wisdom dawns, and they find each other on a remote hill called *Arafat*, the Mount of Mercy. Such joy of meeting! It is the joy of the soul reuniting with its Lord, and with itself.

Surrendered again into Divine Accord, they are led to a nearby valley, "ground turning green beneath their feet as they pass." There, lifting their eyes they behold the heavenly throne with countless angels circling in adoration. Just as the heart is the center of the body, so is this place to which they have come the central place of the world, center of the four directions, the four elements, *the place of union*. There they build the first altar, the original house of prayer. The valley is called *Mecca,* which in Babylonian means "sacred house."

VIEW FROM THE MOUNT OF MERCY

Coming together, creating this shrine, Adam and Eve embody the resolution of conflict, the mystical union of opposites. In the language of symbols, this union is often represented by a *female* downward-pointing triangle interlocked with an upward-pointing *male* triangle. The star formed is a universal emblem of the harmonious heart.

Eventually the shrine is swept away. Ages pass, but this is a place of destiny and prophets, and so it is that in the strength of their days Abraham and his son Ishmael come to the valley of the Sacred House and rebuild the sanctuary. Generations come and go. By the time of Muhammad, the house of the Holy One is filled with a jumble of tribal idols. Muhammad is the *Rasul,* light of the heart, dispeller of differences. His is the task of cleansing the Kaaba and restoring its pristine emptiness, the emptiness only *the One of Infinite Grace and Incomparable Love* can fill.

Turning to the Kaaba in prayer means *turning to the center*, to the place of mystic union, the refuge, to the only place that is *the same in you as it is in me.* For one who understands, the heart is the Kaaba. For those who do not understand, the Kaaba is a proof, that they may someday understand.

THE KAABA

Abraham constructed this building, revealed it
as a place for the Remembrance of Allah
    —as an outward example.

Wherever those with spotlessly pure hearts
replendent with Allah congregate
    —that is the Kaaba.

Wherever everyone gathers in unity
    —that is the Kaaba.

Any place Satan cannot approach
    —that is the Kaaba.

Where the purity and power of Allah intermingle
    —that is the Kaaba.

Where *Beginning, Is Now,* and *Ever Shall Be* meet
    —that is the Kaaba.

The place where you find your unity with Allah
    —that is the Kaaba.

The place where our prayer unites with Allah
    —that is the Kaaba.

—Bawa Muhaiyaddeen

Shams of Tabriz said,   *"The Kaaba is in the middle of the world.*
    All faces turn toward it. Take it away, See!
    each is worshiping the soul of each."

Call Me and I shall answer

Salat

Standing before God

We have heard the Call and heard it repeated. With simple dignity we turn toward the Direction, the *qibla,* and step onto the prayer mat, and out of the ordinary world. Here is the domain of inner need, the refuge where the demands and cares of life lose their grip.

Shoulders relaxed, arms hanging naturally at your side, posture balanced, easy, grounded. Feet slightly apart. The Prayer embraces body as well as spirit in common cause. Breathe easily. Eyes are downcast. The gaze is indrawn, resting lightly on the point of the carpet or mat or earth where forehead will meet the ground in prostration. Find yourself in a state of humility.

Humility is the doorway to the secrets of the heart, humility knows the "I" is an illusion, knows it's a smoke-and-mirrors affair endlessly struggling to project an appearance of solidity.

Humility means seeing our lives as games, our games as trivial, our triumphs as temporary. It means abandoning here on the prayer mat all that we thought that we were and knew. If we want to understand the meaning of humility, we might search out the strength of the servant, not the whining and resentful servant, but the strong and willing one whose strength comes from helping others and in serving a Master who shines with the light of a million suns.

Lo, I am with you always means
when you look for God,
God is in the look of your eyes,
in the thought of looking,
nearer to you than your self,
or things that have happened to you.
There's no need to go outside.

Be melting snow.
Wash yourself of yourself.

THE SETTING OF INTENTION

Raise your hands with palms upward in a pose that evokes both supplication and the receiving of bounty. Move into a state of readiness and one-pointed concentration. We are reaffirming our intention to step into God's embrace. Recite:

In the Name of God,
Boundlessly Merciful and Compassionate!
Bismillah ir Rahman ir Raheem

Clear away all possibilities except the possibility that we can move into the Radiance.

Formal intention includes these simple commitments:
—to perform a certain number of *rakkats,* or cycles, according to the time of prayer.
—to turn toward the *qibla,* the Direction of Prayer.
—to do this only for the sake of the Lord, the Beloved, the inner heart.
—to take refuge in the Beloved from gossip and anger and hatred and all the snares that separate and delude us.

The rest of the intention rises from the heart.

The graceful, rhythmic movements that follow are not an accompaniment to The Prayer, they are The Prayer itself, a mysterious flow of form through which God praises God. We will move through two cycles of prayer although each time has its own number. Additional cycles were recommended by the Prophet and it is traditional to include them.

DAWN PRAYER (Fajr) is two cycles aloud.
NOON PRAYER (Zuhr) is four cycles in silence.
AFTERNOON PRAYER (Asr) is four cycles in silence.
EVENING PRAYER (Maghrib) is two cycles aloud, one silently.
NIGHT PRAYER (Isha) is two cycles aloud, two silently.

As salt dissolves in ocean,
I was swallowed up in you,
beyond doubt or being sure.

Suddenly here in my chest a star
came out so clear, it drew
all stars into it.

THE RECOGNITION OF GOD

Raise hands up with palms open and facing forward. Women raise their hands to the level of their shoulders; men raise them level with their ears.

With this beautiful gesture of transformation, all worldly attachment is pushed behind us. *Readiness* becomes *spiritual alertness.* With our open palms expressing total receptivity to Divine Presence, we say:

God is the Greatest!
Allahu Akbar!

Allahu Akbar! is a joyous bursting forth of exaltation and praise; an affirmation, a sudden intuition that God is not an abstract idea, not the "greatest of all things," but the *source of greatness,* a mighty and unimaginable fortress. So great, God is also smallest, subtlest, all penetrating, all pervasive, the hidden *and* the manifest, the doer, the seer, and the seen.

Muhammad said, *"Don't theorize about Essence!"* All speculations *are* just more layers of covering. Human beings love coverings!

They think the designs on the curtains are what's being concealed.

Observe the wonders as they occur around you. Don't claim them. Feel the artistry moving through, and be silent.

Or say, "I cannot praise You as You should be praised.

Such words are infinitely beyond my understanding."

The Fatiha, or Opener (Men)

Men join their hands over the abdomen, right over left, creating a quiet restraint on this powerful energy center (called the hara in the martial arts). Recite:

> I seek refuge in God, from the darkness of evil
> *Audhu billahi mina-shaitan ir rajim*
> In the Name of God, Source of Mercy and Compassion
> *Bismillah ir Rahman ir Raheem*

Now the Fatiha, the first sura of the Quran is recited. It is a sonic opener of inner worlds, mystically encompassing the entire Quran in seven lines. God needs no praise or plea from us, yet praise lifts the heart from the bondage of self-will into union with the Beloved. Recite:

> All praise is of You, O Lord of all Universes,
> Boundlessly Gracious and Merciful.
> O Master of the Day of Judgment,
> Thee alone do we worship
> And Thine aid we do seek.
> Guide us upon the straight Way,
> The Way of those on whom Thou has bestowed Thy grace,
> Those whose portion is not wrath, and who go not astray. Amen.

> *Alhamdu lillahi Rabbil alamin*
> *Ar-Rahman Ir-Raheem*
> *Maliki yawm-id-din*
> *Iyyaka nabudu wa iyyaka nasta-in*
> *Ihdinas siratal mustaqin*
> *Sirat allathina an amta alaihim*
> *Ghairil maghdubi alaihim wa la dallin.*
> *Amin.*

During the first two rakkats, the Fatiha is followed by the recitation of a passage (containing at least three lines) or a chapter of revelation. These additional passages are not recited in the third and fourth rakkats.

Selections from the Quran are given in the last chapter.

THE FATIHA, OR OPENER (WOMEN)

Various schools of Salat have developed. In some of them women clasp their hands over the heart center of the chest, right over left. See how this most tender of initiatory gestures stirs the *qalb,* or inner heart, the abode of Jesus, the soul of humanity. Angels and madonnas are often painted in this pose.

There is nothing between us and the mysteries of divinity. Recite the Fatiha, and at least three more lines of revelation.

THE BOW

Bow at the waist until the back is parallel to the ground. Hands come down to rest lightly on knees, fingers are spread. Knees are straight. Eyes gaze down at the point that the forehead will touch in prostration. With a simple motion our body imbibes its first taste of submission. This position has been likened to a cow grazing in a storm, so concentrated on nourishment it is oblivious to the rain beating on its back. Recite three times:

Glory to the Lord, the Magnificent One
Subhana Rabbil-Azim

This is a profound meditation on the quality of *magnificence*. When we behold magnificence in the natural world, our response is spontaneous praise. In this emotion is a trail we can follow to its source. Magnificence in the world is like a stained-glass window. Its glory is not in bits of colored glass, but in the light streaming through. Allah, the Creator-Sustainer-Dissolver, Light-of-a-Million-Suns, is the magnificence behind *all* magnificence.

Whatever the devotee is looking for, he is that himself.
How can a lover be anything but the beloved?

Every second he's bowing into a mirror.
If he could see for just a second one molecule
of what's there without fantasizing about it,
he'd explode.
His imagination, and he himself,
would vanish, with all his knowledge, obliterated
into a new birth, a perfectly clear view,
a voice that says, I am God.

That same voice told the angels to bow to Adam,
because they were identical with Adam.

It's the voice that first said,
There is no Reality, but God.
There is only God.

THE PRAISE

As you begin rising to an upright position, recite:

> The Lord hears the one who praises
> *Sami Allahu liman hamidah*

When you have fully risen, arms naturally at your sides and eyes still fixed on the prayer mat, recite these words of gratitude:

> Our Lord! Yours is the praise!
> *Rabbana lakal hamd*

Then, as you begin dropping into the prostration, recite:

> God is the Greatest!
> *Allahu Akbar!*

and continue on to this position of total trust.

> Sometimes you hear a voice through
> the door calling you, as a fish out of
>
> water hears the surf's *come back.*
>
> This turning toward what you deeply
> love saves you. Children fill their
>
> shirts with rocks and carry them
> around. We're not children anymore.
>
> Read the book of your life that has
> been given you. A voice comes to
>
> your soul saying, *Lift your foot,*
> *cross over, move into the emptiness*
> *of question and answer and question.*

THE PROSTRATION

Drop gracefully to your knees, and in an unbroken flow of movement, reach forward and with great care place your hands, then forehead on the ground in prostration. Hands are beside the head, arms are lifted up at the elbows, not resting on the floor. *Our gnostic eye comes to earth.* The gates of Paradise tremble: This is the moment of surrender, the abandonment of the ego. Recite three times:

Glory to the Lord Most Supreme!
Subhana Rabbiyal A'ala

What the world needs now is not more religion and dogmas but a stream—a torrent of warm heart-melt that cuts through the ice cap of our mental hardness. God surely reveals Himself to all who can prostrate themselves before His unknowable reality. Can we give ourselves over to the possibility that we, *too,* are something so marvelous that no one has ever been able to say it? Something so outrageous that knees could actually give way. We could drop to the ground, fall prostrate, fall within the center of the word *humility,* and disappearing, live within it.

The humbling, uplifting power of prostration is understood in all the great religious traditions. Some Tibetan monks must perform 100,000 prostrations before receiving the inner teachings.

THE KNEELING

Conclude your prostration, and recite:

Allahu Akbar!

as you draw back up into a kneeling position. For a moment
stay steady and silent as a mountain, awake, both grounded
and reaching up to the heavens. In such a state, we probe
with utter honesty into our lives, and histories, and thoughts
for the worst that we are. Then turn to the source of mercy,
and ask for forgiveness. Recite three times:

Forgive me, O my Lord
Astagh-firallah al' Athim

Be suspicious of yourself! Inquire

about your hidden motives. It takes courage
to repent, and more courage to change.

But realize this: just as dust grains shine
in sunlight coming through this window,

so there's a light of reality, within which ideas,
hidden hypocrisies, and the qualities

of every action become clear. All you've done
and will do will be seen in the light of that sun.

•••

Lead us.
When we're totally surrendered to that beauty,

we'll become a mighty kindness.

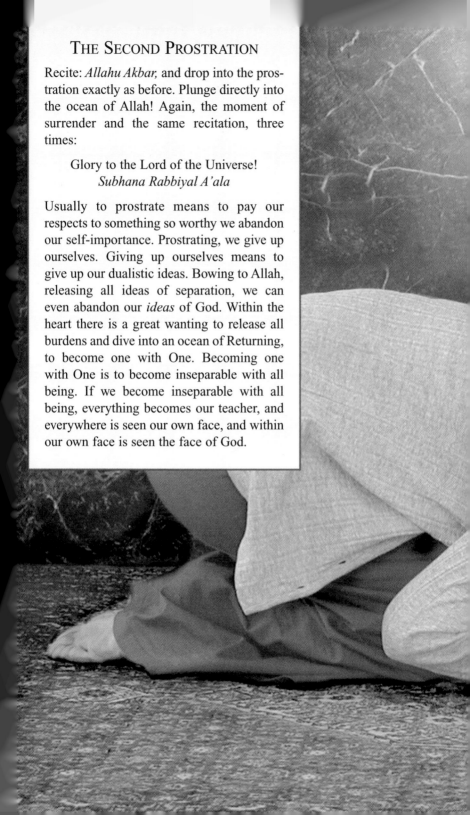

THE SECOND PROSTRATION

Recite: *Allahu Akbar,* and drop into the prostration exactly as before. Plunge directly into the ocean of Allah! Again, the moment of surrender and the same recitation, three times:

Glory to the Lord of the Universe!
Subhana Rabbiyal A'ala

Usually to prostrate means to pay our respects to something so worthy we abandon our self-importance. Prostrating, we give up ourselves. Giving up ourselves means to give up our dualistic ideas. Bowing to Allah, releasing all ideas of separation, we can even abandon our *ideas* of God. Within the heart there is a great wanting to release all burdens and dive into an ocean of Returning, to become one with One. Becoming one with One is to become inseparable with all being. If we become inseparable with all being, everything becomes our teacher, and everywhere is seen our own face, and within our own face is seen the face of God.

POINTING TO THE ONE

Recite: *Allahu Akbar,* and rise to standing, completing one cycle, or *rakkat* of prayer. Every prayer is at least two rakkats, the second is as the first, ending in a kneeling. After two rakkats, we enter the presence of the great prophetic lineage; each prophet a perfection in the stages of spiritual evolution. Recite:

All blessings and acts are sanctified by You, O my Lord.
Peace be upon you, O Messenger of my heart, and the mercy of God and His blessings as well. Peace be on us and on every pilgrim on the path of self-abandonment.

*At-tahi yatu lil lahi was-salawatu wat-tay-yibatu
As-salamu alaika ay-yuhan nabiyyu
Warahmatul-lahi wabarakatuhu
As-salamu alaina wa ala ibadil-lahis salihin*

Lift the index finger of the right hand. Point straight toward the Direction of Prayer, toward the One, and reaffirm the great covenant first heard chanted in the Call:

I bear witness that there is no reality but God.
Ashhadu a-la illaha il Allah.

I bear witness that Muhammad is His servant and messenger.
Wa-ash hadu anna Muhammadan abduhu wa Rasulullah.

Then evoke blessings upon the prophetic lineage, joining a glorious procession of soul-messengers. Recite:

O Allah! Shower Your blessings on our guide Muhammad and those who walk with him on the path of truth, as You showered Your blessings on our guide Abraham and those who walk on his path of unity. Truly, O my Lord, You are the One worthy of praise, the Glorious.

Allahumma salli ala sayyidiina Muhammadin wa ala sayyidina Muhammadin kama sallaita ala sayyidina Ibrahima wa ala ali sayyidina Ibrahim innaka Hamidun Majeed.

To the awakened guide, the succession of prophets is not an event in the realm of long ago and far away. Their vitality is more than mythological, historical, or symbolic. They are experienced directly in the present as blazing lights in the vast firmament of human *Being*. They are grand transformations in the mystical dimension that all humanity participates in. To invoke blessings upon them is to affirm and invigorate our own highest wisdom-nature, to create a living continuity between our inner being and the evolutionary process.

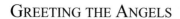

GREETING THE ANGELS

It is said that when we stand in prayer, angels pray also, spreading the merit to the farthest horizons. As a seal to our devotions, we give greetings to this invisible congregation, particularly the angelic awarenesses recording our qualities in thought and deed. We turn our heads to the right and left, reciting each time:

Peace and blessings of God be upon you.
As-salamu alaikum wa rahmatulah.

Are angels real? More than once, after a spontaneous welling up of song, Bawa would remark *what a great number had come.* Not us, he meant the *light-beings* who had hastened to listen: angels and others, invisible to our eyes, not to his, all attracted to the truth-field of a fully enlightened human.

There is a hierarchy:
  human over animal, angel over
  human, and true human beings, the sheikhs,
  the teachers, are above angels.
Why else would the angels be commanded
to bow before Adam?
Does a rose bow to a thorn?
Let your soul follow a one-pointed,
perfected human as thread follows needle.

THE HEART-EMBRACE
UNITY IS THE ESSENCE OF THIS PRAYER

A mystery: After the riches of Salat, the greatest treasure of all comes last, at the very end, in the simplest act of all. We stand and take each other's hand and look into each other's face, looking with the eye that sees the radiance of God within another, sees one's self in another. Embrace gently, saying MAY THE PEACE OF GOD BE UPON YOU, *Asalaam aleikum,* to which the other replies, AND MAY THE PEACE OF GOD BE UPON YOU AS WELL, *Aleikum salaam.* And, following the original instructions from the time of the Holy Prophet, we give this embrace first to those immediately beside us, and then to all who have joined us in prayer, friend and stranger alike.

Only in embracing all
can we become the arms of God.

There is one bright Truth illuminating all religion, and these words and pictures have tried to honor a powerful spiritual technology that expresses it. The Prayer is embraced by millions of people as a living link with the divine. Its formal practice is many-layered, and these introductory instructions invite the seeker to deeper levels of understanding. Those drawn to more complete instructions are directed to the works of Bawa Muhaiyaddeen and Jellaludin Rumi, and other wise masters with knowledge of the ways of prayer beyond the limits of this book.

The beginnings of prayer are the yearnings of the imprisoned heart.

GETTING
doors open
one after another
is the essence of prayer
Every door is a passage, another boundary we have to go beyond.

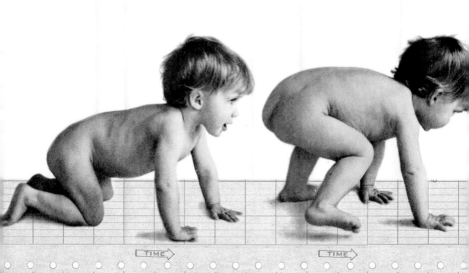

queeze ourselves through, and then go.

FARTHER

TIME

After all,
the purpose of The Prayer
is not to stand and bow
all day long.

The purpose
is to possess continuously
that fragrant state
which appears to you
in prayer.

Asleep or awake,
writing or reading,
in every state
never be empty
of remembrance.

Be rather one of those
moving constantly
within prayer.

CONSTANT PRAYER

The constant prayer of the Sufis is the practice of *Silent Dhikr,* which was root and blossom of Bawa Muhaiyaddeen's wisdom teaching. Dhikr (or Zikr) means "remembrance of God." Among Sufi orders it is often a generalized term for a wide variety of chanting practices. But it is actually a unique act, a unique way of remembering. Not like remembering some important information, it is more *remembering that you exist,* and that your existence *is in unbroken continuity with the existence of God.*

Bawa called this *the Dhikr of the Innermost Heart, the Chant of Reality,* and its transmission turns on a paradox: Doing nothing, we remain in darkness, yet there is nothing we can *do* to bring us to God. This *doing is the problem.* Doing is how empires are built, Olympic medals are won, and trains are kept running on time—*and the idea of an ego-self, a doer, is reinforced.* Approaching the Great and Mysterious One requires a whole other *kind* of movement, a nondoing, an undoing, a melting.

What then? Though we seek Thy-Will, not-my-will, *many-branched and endless is the path of one with little will.* In the end, we need practices. We have work to do, grinding and smoothing and opening—if only to polish ourselves thin enough that light can shine through or exhaust ourselves to the point where the one thing left is surrender.

Bawa's method of teaching Silent Dhikr reflected this paradox. It was not a simple package, another thing *to do.* It was the *Dhikr in which duality ceases to exist.* It was the marriage of sun and moon, of word and breath. It was a passageway opened by the grace of the Qutb.

A flower can only give its own fragrance, is this not so?

Only jasmine can give the fragrance of jasmine.

  The fragrance of Allah can only
  be given by Allah.

That is true prayer.

In the way of what can be said and taught, here is the teaching. May some fragrance of grace be here as well!

Silent Dhikr begins with contemplation of the First Kalima, first heard in the call to prayer:

LA ILLAHA, IL ALLAHU

Kalima means *word, aphorism,* or *authority,* and this formulation compresses with poetic brevity a vast wealth of information about the true nature of reality and our relationship with it. Word-by-word translation is cryptic: *Not-infinite-if-not-God.* But Arabic words always have a wide range of meanings. The usual rendering, *There is no god but God,* is somewhat vague. The poetic *There is no reality but God* goes deeper, hinting that things are not always what they seem. But Bawa's initiatory *The "I" is an illusion; God alone is Real* touches secrets. A friend once asked Bawa to explain. For three days, the master tried to communicate a direct understanding of reality. Finally, frustrated by the limitations of language, he declared:

THE CAR IS GOING DOWN THE ROAD BUT THE ROAD IS INSIDE THE CAR!

THE BREATH WITHIN BREATH

having begun contemplation of the Kalima, we now open our attention to include our breathing. With pure observation only, witness your breath, making no attempt at control. The human body is a complex spiritual instrument. Ordinary physical breathing is not only the exchange of oxygen and carbon dioxide, it is a link to our light body. With every inhale-exhale, a parallel energy flow in our light body is occurring. Bringing attention to the outer breath cultivates a growing awareness of this inner breath, harmonizes these interpenetrating bodies, and quiets the mind. *In breath the visible and invisible worlds meet.*

Truth seekers of every tradition have studied this phenomenon. *"What we call 'I',"* said Zen master Suzuki Roshi, *"is just a swinging door which moves when we inhale and when we exhale. It just moves; that is all. When your mind is pure and calm enough to follow this movement, there is nothing: no 'I,' no world, no mind or body; just a swinging door."*

Various healing systems have developed sophisticated maps of this other anatomy and its energy paths. Ayurvedic medicine knows 72,000 subtle nerves called nadis; acupuncture has mapped the meridians. The profound Silent Dhikr of the Qutb awakens these pathways.

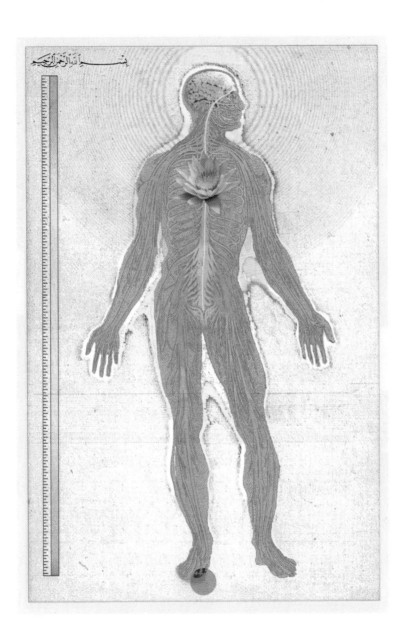

The Holy Prophet said:
May divine light be before me, behind me, to the right and left, above and below.
May my limbs be filled with divine light. May my skin be filled with divine light.

119

Now the Kalima is joined with breath. LA ILLAHA moves with and empowers *exhalation* and IL ALLAHU moves with and activates *inhalation*. We discover that with every outer breath, an inner breath is engaged in an ongoing gnostic process, alternating between a self-surrendering exhale and a God-embracing inhale. Purification and glorification. *Death and birth.* The Kalima's *insights become experience.* This is the original breath of the harmonious human being. The noble prophet M u h a m m a d said, *For everything there is a polish which takes away rust, and the polish of the heart is Dhikr.*

This current of the Dhikr, the remembrance of God, is something we discover, not create. It is always flowing in and out with the breath like a secret tide.

This current of the Dhikr, the remembrance of God, is something we discover, not create. It is always flowing in and out with

ilaha ilAllah

Literal	Not Infinite	If not God
Traditional	There is no god	But God
Poetic	There is no reality	But God
Initiatory	The "I" is an illusion	God alone is Real
Breath	In breath, left side	Out breath, right side
Polarity	Negation	Affirmation
Function	Outflowing illusion	Indrawing grace
Movement	Contraction	Expansion
Intention	Dispersion	Surrender
Quality	Lunar/Reflected Conditioned	Solar/Original Essence

THE PATH OF THE DHIKR

LA ILLAHA
The Moon Breath
The Outflowing Breath

IL ALLAHU
The Sun Breath
The Inflowing Breath

Along with the natural outbreath directed through the left nostril, your unswerving concentration should draw the words la illaha—*Other than You nothing is real,* from the ends of the toes upward through all the tissues of the body, the heart, and up to the *arsh,* the throne of God at the crown of the head, then down and exhaled. The breath rises with this sound, and like murky water being suctioned from a silted well, carries everything along with it: the karma of our birth, the false impressions of the five senses, our faults and self-delusions, seductive energies and obsessions and attachments and base desires belonging to the lower world and every limitation the mind has gathered to itself. Within the vibration of la illaha, the analytic wisdom of the Qutb filters everything, discarding whatever is not of the soul. In this way the soul is purified with every breath.

Breathing in through the right nostril, this is the breath known as the sun breath, the *breath of love* that causes the heart to bloom in compassion. When an overwhelming yearning for truth arises in the heart, it becomes a magnet, drawing to itself a current of luminous living sunlike Presence. On this breath-current rides the weighty words il Allahu, *You are the One,* and it flows up to the gnostic eye at the center of the forehead, the seat of divine knowledge. It pauses here, causing a pressure, then rises to the crown and spreads out through the brain. Then the current descends to the inner heart, the qalb, as *hu,* the resonance of God, "*O God, You alone are Real,*" and merges with the soul. Our connections are now turned on, current flows everywhere within, illuminating all the universes. This is the point where *Two* ceases and *One* begins.

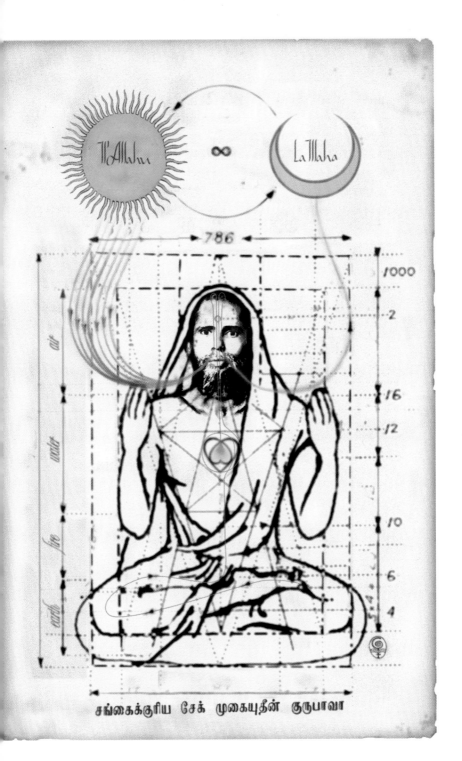

சங்கைக்குரிய சேக் முகையுதீன் குருபாவா

Bawa continually reminded us that this was the essential work of the Sufi path:

AY LA ILLAHA IL ALLAHU. Don't waste your breath. With every breath, say LA ILLAHA IL ALLAHU.

It must be said with your breath. You don't have to make a sound; your tongue silently repeating: La Illaha, nothing is real; Il Allahu, only God exists—and planted firmly within the qalb, your inner heart.

"Whatever time it is or whatever place you may be, whether you are walking or sitting or working or sleeping—at all times this breath must flow continually. Both the in and out movements must be clearly understood. Its sounds, its meanings, its lights—everything should be understood in Divine Luminous Wisdom. Say it like this. Do not even waste even one second!

"All states of consciousness must unite together and recite these words. Whatever work you are doing, it is good if you keep on reciting like this. Always remember to recite it like this.

"It must go on like this. His actions—the actions of God—must be acquired. Become the duty of God. Say it like this. Whatever you may be doing, this work should go on. These words must go on resonating in your heart.

"This Prayer must go on! The work of uniting with God must be done!

"When you come here to listen to wisdom, even at the time of listening you should still be doing this work. This is the most important work you can do. All the time it must go on. It is only then that the seedlings will grow. Then only will the light resplend. Only then will unity become apparent. Only then can we unite with God and do His will.

"Make yourself aware, and by making yourself aware you will make others aware. Do it like this. Don't waste your time. We have very little time left!

"My sons—my daughters! This is the pure word! It is on the left and it is on the right:

Other than God there is nothing;
God alone Exists.

In this way you are in unity with the Eternal One."

(From a longer discourse)

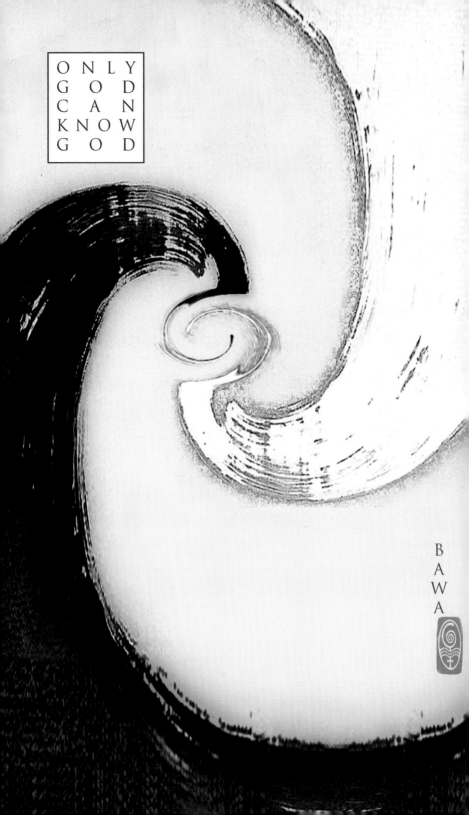

ONLY
GOD
CAN
KNOW
GOD

LY
D
A
N
W
D

BAWA

The Qutb approached the mystery of Silent Dhikr from every dimension. Sometimes it was a not: *not* a prayer, *not* a meditation. Sometimes the flow of its energy through the body was catalogued in microscopic detail. Or Dhikr was words repeated inwardly. I asked if the Dhikr must be recited in Arabic and was told it could be Arabic or English, *but Dhikr isn't words at all.* The mind demands clear directions, but mystical understanding always slips through conceptual nets. Truth prefers metaphor. *Like the glimmer of light on water, like the sound of one hand clapping.*

The practice of this Silent Dhikr is circular, but it is not a mantra, not magical vibratory sound patterns evoking elemental energies. It is not associated with any deities or powers or presences, except the presence of the Great Mystery, That-by-which-all-else-is-known. Silent Dhikr is a matter of longing and remembrance, of submission to remembrance, of guiding breath, of surrendering to the great spaciousness of the soul, sliding into the sea of light.

...sten to it, as the personal self breaks open.

SURRENDER

Silent Dhikr is a drawing of the curtains, an invitation into the secret gardens of submission, a small blue doorway suddenly opening into a great chamber. Entering, we must let ourselves be absorbed by what the early followers of Jesus called the *Cloud of Unknowing*. One of the most graphic and challenging depictions of such submission is the Buddhist image of a female supplicant being utterly possessed by a powerful flashing-eyed deity. This bizarre and dreamlike vision imparts a fleeting sense of what it is to raise the flag of unconditional surrender at the "embrace" of *al-Aziz,* God-the-Mighty, or *al-Fatah,* God-the-Opener. Of course, the Ground of Being can never be depicted, but sometimes images, like sunsets, tell a worthy God-story. Rumi often depicted the infinite as an intimate lover or Friend:

I would love to kiss you.
The price of kissing
       is your life.
Now my loving is
       running
toward my life
       shouting,

What a bargain!
Let's buy it!

Not · I · but · Thou!

We are moving into a new course of study, away from the certainties of *acquired* knowledge and into the mysterious work of *knowing ourselves*.

This study is both the most difficult and easiest of all pursuits. *Difficult* because it doesn't fall under the supervision of our familiar *Department of External Studies . . .*

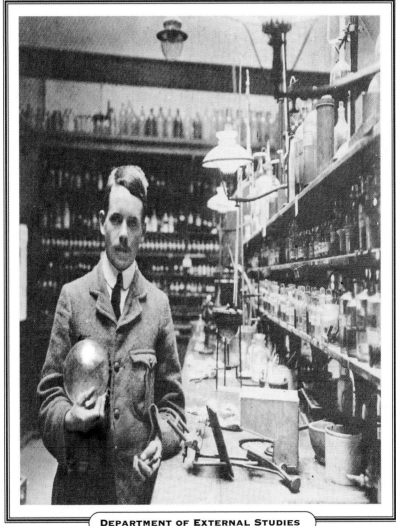

DEPARTMENT OF EXTERNAL STUDIES

Easy because it is a study of that which is *most* familiar: our own consciousness, that by which all else is known. It is also near, no farther than *the awareness reading this book.*

FINAL STEPS
Understand all external phenomena as manifestations
of internal phenomena.

The fragrance of the Dhikr finally must penetrate all our actions. If *God alone is real,* then all people and situations must be perceived as partaking of the divine and therefore not separate from ourselves. If the "I" is melted away, abandoned— if only for an instant—then for that instant we become divine action in the world. God's gesture is our gesture, the Great Compassion is our compassion, our mercy can be *most merciful.* Our lives become the Dhikr in action.

Let the beauty we love
be what we do.
There are hundreds of ways to kneel
in prayer.

*I*n every action that we do,

in everything we do,

we should treat each other

with the *soft hand.*

Not the callused hand

of the woodcutter,

but the soft hand of the flower

anpu, the inner flower of the heart.

God is a Power

The power becomes light

The light becomes vibration

The vibration becomes sound

The sound becomes word

The word becomes language

The language becomes scripture.

Like that

RETURN TO THE SOURCE

—Bawa Muhaiyaddeen

The Recitations

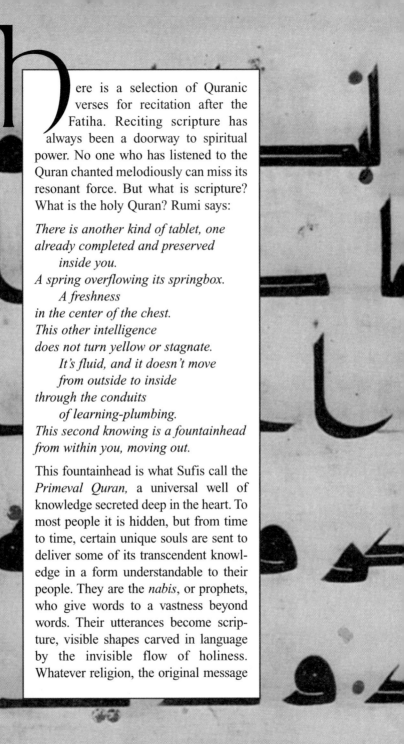

ere is a selection of Quranic verses for recitation after the Fatiha. Reciting scripture has always been a doorway to spiritual power. No one who has listened to the Quran chanted melodiously can miss its resonant force. But what is scripture? What is the holy Quran? Rumi says:

There is another kind of tablet, one
already completed and preserved
     inside you.
A spring overflowing its springbox.
     A freshness
in the center of the chest.
This other intelligence
does not turn yellow or stagnate.
     It's fluid, and it doesn't move
     from outside to inside
through the conduits
     of learning-plumbing.
This second knowing is a fountainhead
from within you, moving out.

This fountainhead is what Sufis call the *Primeval Quran,* a universal well of knowledge secreted deep in the heart. To most people it is hidden, but from time to time, certain unique souls are sent to deliver some of its transcendent knowledge in a form understandable to their people. They are the *nabis*, or prophets, who give words to a vastness beyond words. Their utterances become scripture, visible shapes carved in language by the invisible flow of holiness. Whatever religion, the original message is the same: *Come into the heart, where the Great Mystery lives! Look, here is the Way.*

These soul-mentors have come to all peoples, and when Muhammad emerged, a distinctive cycle of revelation that had flowed through 124,000 previous messengers was completed.

The sacred languages—Sanskrit, Greek, Hebrew, Arabic, and others—are distinguished by a unity between a word's sound and its meaning. Without knowing a language we can often understand a word, as in *Ahh-LAAAH,* the Arabic word for God. Its vowels roll out softly from deep in the back of the throat, a universal cry of longing. Translation dilutes intensity, and transmissions from a higher dimension are clearest in the language delivered. In orthodox practice Quranic passages are always recited aloud in Arabic. However most readers will not only be unfamiliar with Arabic—their *yearning* is in English. Bawa would tell a story about parrot-work:

*Don't recite words you've learned by rote
and think you're praying.*
 That's parrot work.
*If a cat comes, what does the parrot say?
"Help! A cat approaches?" No,
it will squawk and screech, completely
forgetting its prayer-performance!*
 *Yearning for God in every thought,
directing every breath toward the One,
intending no harm,*
  that is prayer.

These passages are given first in English. Rather than calling them *translations*, with a sense of finality, think of them as *meditations*, a process the reader is invited to join.

EARLY VERSION OF THE WRITTEN QURAN
C. EIGHTH–NINTH CENTURY

RECITATIONS

After the Sura Fatiha, which is recited standing during each rakkat of prayer, a passage of revelation is recited. Many let the choice come spontaneously to their heart. The primary requirement is that it should speak to your life. Here are three potent, compact suras.

Sura Ikhlas, or Purity of Faith

In the name of God, Most Gracious, Most Merciful
Say: He is God
The One and Only;
God, the Eternal, Absolute;
He begetteth not; nor is He begotten;
And there is none like unto Him.

Bismillah ir Rahman ir Raheem
Qul: Huwallahu ahad
Allahu Samad
Lam yalid, wa lam yulad
Walam yakul-lahu kufuwan ahad.

The Sura Ikhlas is so vital that it is said to be equivalent to one-third of the Quran. Its simplicity holds infinite depth. This is the prayer of the heart that wants nothing other than Allah and is lost forever in the boundless light of Ahad, The One: "He is Allah, the One and Only Reality, the All-Encompassing who does not originate from some other reality. Nor does anything originate separate from Him. Apart from Him, there is absolutely nothing. He is Oneness Alone. Fragmentation, false appearances, and separations are all dissolved in the light of certainty."

The Mazar, or shrine, of Bawa Muhaiyaddeen, *may God sanctify his secret*. Throughout the Sufi world, Mazars are known as places of remembrance, healing, and pilgrimage.

Two Verses of Protection:

SURA FALAQ, OR DAYBREAK

In the name of God, Most Gracious, Most Merciful
Say: I seek refuge in the Lord of the Dawn,
From the deception within created things;
From the mischief of those who misuse secret knowledge,
And from the snares of the envious nature as it practices envy.

Bismillah ir Rahman ir Raheem
Qul auzu birabil falaq
Min sharri ma khalaq
Wa min sharri ghasiqin iza waqab
Wa min sharrin naffasati fil uqad
Wa min sharri hasidin iza hasad

The understanding:
"I seek true refuge with the Lord of perpetually dawning Wisdom—from the darkness of despair; fear, and uncertainty that is generated by limited conscious beings, by magic practices and superstition, and from the disturbances of envy."

Sura Nas, or Humankind

In the name of God, Most Gracious, Most Merciful
Say: I seek refuge in the Lord and Cherisher of
                              humankind,
The Mystic Sovereign of humankind,
The God of humankind,
From the mischief of the whispering, elusive tempter
Whispering in the human heart
And from (the temptations) of intangible spirit beings,
                              as well as men.

Bismillah ir Rahman ir Raheem
Qul auzu bi-Rabbin nas
Malikin nas
Illahin nas
Min sharril waswassil khanas
Allathi yuwaswisu fi-sudurin nas
Minal jinnati wan-nas.

The understanding:
"I seek refuge in the Lord and Cherisher of
humankind, the Mystic Sovereign of humankind, the
God of humankind, from the invisible forces of
nature that affect our psyche and confuse and tempt
us into wrongdoing, and from the promptings of the
impure heart that incite divisiveness. And from the
subtle influences of intangible elemental spirits, as
well as the ill wishes that can flow from men."

THIS LOVE

IS UNIQUE

AND UNTO ITSELF.

AS FLOWER

AND

FRAGRANCE

ARE JOINED

TOGETHER,

SO OUR

LOVE AND

GOD'S LOVE

SHOULD JOIN.

—BAWA

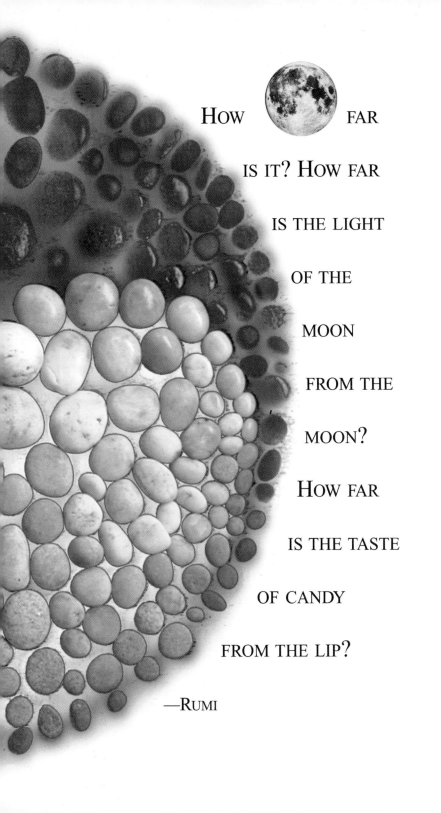

How FAR IS IT? HOW FAR IS THE LIGHT OF THE MOON FROM THE MOON? HOW FAR IS THE TASTE OF CANDY FROM THE LIP?

—RUMI

If they are any mistakes in this book, please forgive us. They are ours and not our guides'. We have tried to pass on subtle understandings that are best conveyed in a living transmission.

The way
a heart finds its way
to the Beloved
is a mysterious matter.

You and I
have spoken all these
words,
but as for the way
we have to go,
words are no preparation.

There's no getting ready,
other than grace.
My faults have
stayed hidden.
One might call that
a preparation!
I have one small drop
of knowing
in my soul.
Let it dissolve
in your ocean.

This book rises flamelike, from the help, and support, and common-sense grounding of a circle of friends. Foremost, my wife, Saliha, whose persevering sensibilities kept this book (we hope) on the delicate edge where formless-ness meets form. And peerless agent Reid Boates, moving with *clean spirit, sharp sword* through the marketplace, and edit-or Leslie Meredith who said *Let there be color,* and lo, there was color. And (in order of appearance), Kabir, Fara of Senegal, Maryam of Jerusalem, Sharaf Atakhanov, Ruth King and Rabia Rose, Larry Didona, Ismailiea Burah, Mary Fatima Boardman, Kabeera McCorkle, Dr. Hochberg, Daniel Abd' al-Hayy Moore, Dr. K. Ganeshan, Saliha, and Jonathan Granoff and Muhammad Abdullah Lowe, hugging so nicely. And Usha Balamore for her good ear for truth. My heartfelt thanks to all, and special gratitude to Coleman for his generosity of spirit and to the Sufi Learning Community and sacred archivists of the Bawa Muhaiyaddeen Fellowship in Philadelphia! This work is an offering to the sublime master Muhammad Raheem Bawa Muhaiyaddeen, who was also Guru Bawa, who was the Qutb that came to the West, may this hidden secret be known. May the Peace and Blessing of God be upon them all, and upon you, the reader, as well!